Following Christ. What's it all about?

Discipleship Explored Handbook (2nd Edition)
Copyright © 2012 Christianity Explored
First published in 2012. Reprinted 2012, 2013, 2014.

www.ceministries.org

Published by
The Good Book Company Ltd

Websites:
UK: www.thegoodbook.co.uk
North America: www.thegoodbook.com
Australia: www.thegoodbook.com.au
New Zealand: www.thegoodbook.co.nz

ISBN: 9781908317438

Design by Steve Devane and André Parker

Printed in the Czech Republic

Contents

Welcome

Over the next eight sessions we will read the book of Philippians to discover how good it is to be a follower of Jesus Christ, and how he calls his disciples to live for him today.

Don't be afraid to ask questions, no matter how simple or difficult you think they are. And if you have to miss a week, don't worry. There is a short summary of the previous session at the start of each study.

CONFIDENT IN CHRIST

1

EXPLORE

🔹 What would you write to your friends if you were unfairly put in prison?

LISTEN

"He who began a good work in you will carry it on to completion until the day of Christ Jesus." (Philippians 1:6)

- Philippians is a letter written by Paul to the Christians living in Philippi, to help them keep going as Christians.

- Paul wrote his letter while in prison in Rome.

- He knew God was working in the Philippians because of their "partnership in the gospel" (Philippians 1:5).

- Paul was confident that God would finish the work of salvation he began.

- We know that God has begun his good work in us if we are living as partners in the gospel, demonstrating our love for Jesus.

- We can be confident that what God starts he finishes.

- "Disciple" means "learner". God will help us learn how to live for him and grow in our knowledge of him.

Notes
Philippians 1:1-11

DISCUSS

1. According to Philippians 1:6, what confidence should we have as Christians?

2. In the middle of daily life, why is verse 6 sometimes hard to believe?

Bible words

Christ/Messiah: God's only chosen King, who God promised to send into the world.

Saints: Those who God has set apart for himself. Every Christian is a saint.

Overseers and deacons: Church leaders.

Grace: God's gift of forgiveness to people who do not deserve it.

Gospel: The good news about Jesus Christ.

Day of Christ: The day when Jesus Christ will return to judge the world.

Righteousness: Goodness that is good enough for God. To be righteous means to be right with God.

3. What can we hold on to when we lack confidence in our salvation?

4. What difference should this confidence make to our lives?

5. What is the result of God's "good work in you" and when will it be complete? (See verses 6, 10, 11.)

FOLLOW UP

Each week, Follow Up gives you a plan to help you read the Bible every day. The passages this week help to explain how we can be confident of our salvation. There's room at the end for any questions you'd like to discuss next time.

SUNDAY

Read the passage that will be preached at the church service you attend.

On the other six days...

DAY ONE

Re-read Philippians 1:1-11

Think about the answers you gave to the Discuss questions on pages 7-8.

Thank God that if he has started any "good work" in you, he will complete it.

DAY TWO

Read 1 John 1:5 – 2:1

John wrote this letter in around 90AD. It is probably a circular letter intended for a number of churches.

1. What is "walking in the light"? (See 1 John 1:6-7.)

(Clue: People who walk in the light need the blood of Jesus to purify them [verse 7] so it can't mean "being perfect". Light reveals things; it helps us to see them clearly. Take a look at John 3:20–21.)

2. So, what is "walking in the darkness"? (See 1 John 1:5-6.)

3. Put verse 8 into your own words.

4. How can we be certain that confessing sin will result in our forgiveness? (See 1 John 1:9.)

5. What is encouraging about the balance in 1 John 2:1?

Spend a few minutes thanking God for the secure faith you have, which is based upon what Jesus has already done for you.

DAY THREE

Read John 6:35-40

These verses are taken from a discussion the crowd is having with Jesus after he miraculously fed over 5000 people with five small loaves and two fish (John 6:1-15). The crowd demands a miraculous sign like the one Moses gave when he fed the Israelites with manna in the wilderness (Exodus 16:11-18, 31).

Jesus reminds them that it was his Father in heaven who fed the people. And in any case, says Jesus, the "true bread" is "he who comes down from heaven and gives life to the world".

1. What "life" does Jesus bring (v 35)?

(Clue: Look at what John 3:16 says about the reason Jesus was sent.)

2. Look at the promise in verse 37. How can you be sure that you are included in this promise?

3. God's plan for us is clearly given in verses 39 and 40.
What is *God's* part in this plan?

➡ What is *our* part?

▨ *Use these verses to thank God for what he is doing in your life and to pray about the coming sessions at* **Discipleship Explored***.*

DAY FOUR

👁 **Read Ephesians 2:8-10**

Paul wrote this letter to the Christians in Ephesus. These verses explain very clearly how we have been saved.

1. According to verses 8 and 9, what is it that saves us?

2. What is it that Paul says has no power to save us?

(Note: He mentions these because it is all too easy to rely on them rather than on God.)

3. Put verse 8 into your own words.

4. Verse 10 is packed with meaning. What are the three things we learn? All three are God-centred and God-initiated.

Pray that God would enable you to rely solely on him.

DAY FIVE

Re-read the Bible passages you've read over the past week. Choose a verse that you found particularly helpful, write it down in the space below and memorize it.

DAY SIX

*Read Philippians 1:12–26 in preparation for **Discipleship Explored**.*

Do you have any questions about the passages you have read this week?

Summary

In the last session we saw that Paul wrote this letter to a group of new Christians living in Philippi to help them keep going as Christians. Paul was confident that whatever happens, God would finish the work of salvation that he began in them. Therefore we can have the same confidence.

LIVING IN CHRIST

EXPLORE

🔲 *Discuss any questions from last session's Follow Up.*

🔲 *Look together at Philippians 1:9-11 and answer the questions below.*

1. What does Paul pray for the Philippian Christians?

2. Why does he pray for these things? (See verse 10.)

3. What does Paul hope will be the result of this? (See verse 11.)

4. How might Paul's prayer shape the way we pray for other Christians?

LISTEN

"For to me, to live is Christ and to die is gain." (Philippians 1:21)

Notes
Philippians 1:12-26

- Paul's circumstances were bad:

    - he wrote his letter from prison.

    - there were people trying to stir up trouble for him.

    - he didn't know if he would live or die.

- But Paul was rejoicing – because he knew that everything that had happened had "served to advance the gospel" (Philippians 1:12).

- The most important thing to Paul was that people were hearing about Jesus.

- Paul taught the Philippians (and us) that: "To live is Christ and to die is gain" (Philippians 1:21).

- There is only one way to live that death cannot touch. That is to live for Christ.

Bible words

Brothers in the Lord: Christians. All Christians are part of God's family.
The Spirit of Jesus Christ: The Holy Spirit. God sends His Spirit to help people who become Christians.

DISCUSS

1. Paul's greatest ambition was for the gospel to spread.
What is your greatest ambition? (Be honest!)

2. What pressures did Paul face that may have led him to put his own desires first? (See Philippians 1:13, 15-17, 23.)

➲ What was his attitude to these pressures and why?

3. How might our circumstances, reputation or future plans affect our desire to tell others about Christ?

4. How would you put Paul's motto in verse 21, "To live is Christ and to die is gain", into your own words?

5. How would your friends or colleagues finish this sentence: "For me to live is…"?

➡ What about you? How would you finish that same sentence?

FOLLOW UP

In Philippians 1:19, Paul tells the Philippian church that he has been helped by their prayers and "the Spirit of Jesus Christ". The passages this week will tell us more about the Holy Spirit and what he does. There's room at the end to write down any questions you'd like to discuss next time.

SUNDAY

Read the passage that will be preached at the church service you attend.

On the other six days...

DAY ONE
Re-read Philippians 1:12-26

Think about the answers you gave to the questions in Discuss on pages 16-17.

Pray that you would be able to echo Paul's motto with conviction: "For to me, to live is Christ and to die is gain".

DAY TWO
Read John 14:15-31

In this passage, Jesus is speaking just hours before his death. He wants the disciples to know that they won't be alone when he leaves them. The Holy Spirit will be given to them, and will be with them for ever.

The word translated "Counsellor" in this passage is literally "one who comes alongside"; an advocate. Jesus promises "*another* Counsellor". Jesus is the first "one who comes alongside" and the Holy Spirit will follow him, so the Holy Spirit is a person. Notice too that in verse 17 the Holy Spirit is referred to as "him" and "he".

1. How does Jesus describe the Holy Spirit in John 14:16?

2. In verses 17-18, what is the difference between "the world's" relationship to the Holy Spirit and ours?

(Note: Jesus describes the relationship between himself, the Father and the Holy Spirit as very close indeed. Jesus says in verse 17 that the *Holy Spirit* is in us, and he also says in verse 20 that *he* – Jesus – is in us.)

3. The main theme in this passage is love (verses 15, 21, 23-24). How is our love for Jesus shown in practice? (See verses 21 and 23.)

4. What is the consequence of living in this way?

Thank God for the work of the Holy Spirit in your life, asking that he would increase your understanding of the Bible. Pray that you would increasingly demonstrate your love for Jesus by obedience (John 14:15).

DAY THREE

Read John 16:5-15

1. What are the three ways in which the Counsellor – the Holy Spirit – "convicts the world"? (See John 16:8.)

2. How does Jesus explain these three in verses 9 to 11?

3. Jesus promises the apostles in verse 13 that the Holy Spirit will guide them into "all truth". How does this promise give us confidence as we read the New Testament? (See also John 14:26.)

It is very important to see that the Holy Spirit's role is to draw attention to Jesus. Read John 16:14-15 again, and also John 15:26.

🔲 *Ask the Holy Spirit to make Jesus more real to you as you read the Bible.*

DAY FOUR

👁 Read Acts 2:1-13

Acts was written by the same Luke who wrote the Gospel. In fact, as you can see from the start of both books, both were originally intended for the same reader, Theophilus.

Acts 2:1–13 records the way in which the Holy Spirit was given to the first Christians on the day of Pentecost. (The Greek word "Pentecost" means "fifty". The day of Pentecost was the fiftieth day after the Sabbath, the Jewish holy day, at the end of Passover week. It was a celebration of the end of the barley harvest and a feast of the "first fruits" of the full harvest.)

1. What was the effect of the disciples being filled with the Holy Spirit? (See verses 4 and 6.)

2. What was it the disciples were saying to the people as they did this? (See verse 11.)

3. Read Genesis 11:1–9. How does this contrast with what happened on the day of Pentecost?

In the Old Testament, the Holy Spirit was only given to people with particular roles – prophets, kings and priests. But Acts 2:17–18 quotes a prophecy from the prophet Joel that, one day, the Holy Spirit would fill every one of God's people, in every nation. The day of Pentecost was the fulfilment of that prophecy.

Spend time praying, thanking God for the Holy Spirit's presence in your life.

DAY FIVE

Re-read the Bible passages you've read over the past week.
Choose a verse that you found particularly helpful, write it down in the space below and memorize it.

DAY SIX

*Read Philippians 1:27 – 2:11 in preparation for **Discipleship Explored**.*

Do you have any questions about the passages you have read this week?

Summary

In the last session we saw that the most important thing in Paul's life was that people were hearing about Jesus. Paul teaches the Philippians (and us) that: "To live is Christ and to die is gain" (Philippians 1:21).

STANDING TOGETHER IN CHRIST

3

EXPLORE

- Discuss any questions from last session's Follow Up.
- Look together at Philippians 1:21-26 and answer the questions below.

1. What dilemma does Paul face?

2. Why does Paul want to "go on living"?

3. What is it about death that Paul finds so attractive? (See verse 23.)

4. Do you share Paul's view of death? Why or why not?

5. What do these verses tell us about Paul's mindset?

LISTEN

"Your attitude should be the same as that of Christ Jesus."
(Philippians 2:5)

Notes
Philippians 1:27 – 2:11

■ Christians are to stand together for the gospel – "in one spirit" and "as one man" (Philippians 1:27).

■ We can't fight for the gospel if we're fighting with each other.

■ Suffering for Christ is a normal experience for a Christian.

■ Our attitude should be the same as that of Jesus.

■ We should consider others better than ourselves. The secret of standing together is humility.

■ Jesus made himself like a slave.

■ One day *every* knee will bow and *every* tongue confess that Jesus Christ is Lord.

Bible words

The gospel of Christ: The good news about Jesus Christ.

DISCUSS

1. According to Philippians 1:27, what does it mean to conduct ourselves "in a manner worthy of the gospel of Christ"?

2. What opportunities do you have to "contend" for the gospel by sharing your faith with others?

3. Paul and the Philippian church faced opposition because they were "contending" for the gospel (see verses 28–30). Why might we face opposition to the gospel today?

4. In verses 28–30 Paul makes some surprising statements. From these verses, what should we remember when we face opposition?

5. What does it mean to stand together, according to Paul in Philippians 2:2?

6. What will it mean in practice for us to "consider others better" than ourselves?

FOLLOW UP

Philippians 2:5–11 gives a wonderful insight into the humility and selflessness of Jesus. The passages this week focus on Jesus and his mission to rescue us from our sin.

SUNDAY

Read the passage that will be preached at the church service you attend.

On the other six days...

DAY ONE

Re-read Philippians 1:27 – 2:11

Think about the answers you gave to the questions in Discuss on pages 26-27.

Pray for strength and wisdom so that, wherever you are, your attitude is "the same as that of Christ Jesus".

DAY TWO

Read Isaiah 53:1-12

These verses, which describe the suffering of God's "servant", were written about 700 years before Jesus was born. It is remarkable that so much of Jesus' mission is prophesied here.

1. Looking at verses 4–6, what similarities can you find between the "servant" and Jesus Christ?

   (Note: "Transgressions" and "iniquities" are another way of describing sin.)

2. What does the servant's suffering achieve?

3. Why is this suffering necessary? (See verse 6.)

4. In Acts 8:26–35, Philip meets an Ethiopian who is reading verses 7–8 of Isaiah 53. How do you think Philip used these verses to tell the Ethiopian "the good news about Jesus" (Acts 8:35)?

5. Read 1 Peter 2:22–25. Which verses from Isaiah 53 can you detect in this passage?

Give thanks to God for the good news of Jesus.

DAY THREE

Read Luke 15:1-32

A parable is a simple story with a spiritual meaning. Verses 1 and 2 tell us the background to these parables. The comment in verse 2 was meant as an insult – but for us it is very good news.

1. What do the three parables tell us about the mission of Jesus and how God views "sinners"?

2. The parable of the lost son has a bit more detail in it than the other two. Verse 20 is a very bold picture of God. What might surprise non-Christians about this verse?

3. Jesus probably intended the religious leaders (who were listening, see verse 2) to see themselves as the older son. What was the older son – and by implication the religious leaders – missing out on?

4. How can we make sure we don't miss out in the same way?

The parable of the lost son is a wonderful picture of the compassion of God and the mission of Jesus.

Thank God for the extraordinary nature of his fatherly compassion for you. Who do you need to have compassion on in your daily life? Pray about this and ask God to give you his compassion for them.

DAY FOUR

Read Colossians 1:15-23

This letter was written by Paul to the Christians living in Colosse, in modern-day Turkey. These verses give us a profound insight into who Jesus is.

1. What does Paul mean when he calls Jesus "the image of the invisible God" (verse 15)? (See verse 19.)

2. Paul also describes Jesus as "the firstborn over all creation".
What does he mean by that, according to verses 16–18?

3. Jesus is described by Paul as:

➔ the one who reveals God

➔ the creator of the universe

➔ the purpose of the universe

➔ the sustainer of everything

➔ the head of the church

➔ the reconciler.

Identify the verses that correspond to these descriptions.

4. In the light of this, what should our attitude be towards Jesus?

5. Because of humankind's rebellion against God (Genesis 3), everything has
been severed from its rightful relationship with the Father and needs to be
reconciled to him. How is this achieved? (See verse 20.)

6. Verse 22 mentions our own reconciliation with God through the death of Jesus. For what purpose have we been reconciled?

7. According to verse 23, what should our response be to this reconciliation?

🔲 *Reflect on the descriptions of Jesus you found in question 3, and praise God for such a mighty Saviour. Pray too that you will "continue in your faith, established and firm, not moved from the hope held out in the gospel".*

DAY FIVE

🔲 *Re-read the Bible passages you've read over the past week. Choose a verse that you found particularly helpful, write it down in the space below and memorize it.*

DAY SIX

🔲 *Read Philippians 2:12-30 in preparation for **Discipleship Explored**.*

Do you have any questions about the passages you have read this week?

Summary

In the last session we saw that we need to stay sure of what we believe and work together for the gospel. This will help us when we face opposition. Our attitude should be like that of Jesus.

TRANSFORMED BY CHRIST

EXPLORE

- *Discuss any questions from last session's Follow Up.*

- *Look together at Philippians 2:5-11 and answer the questions below.*

1. Our attitude "should be the same as that of Christ Jesus" (verse 5). What exactly was Jesus' attitude? (See verses 7–8.)

2. Jesus "did not consider equality with God something to be grasped" (verse 6). Why not?

3. Are there any situations in which a Christian needs to "grasp equality with God"? Why or why not?

4. What were the results of Jesus' attitude, according to verses 9-11?

5. Having read this passage, how can you live "to the glory of God" (verse 11) this week?

LISTEN

"Shine like stars in the universe as you hold out the word of life."
(Philippians 2:15-16)

■ We should "shine like stars" by telling people the gospel, the "word of life".

■ The gospel must shine from *every* part of our lives, not just from what we say.

■ Disciples will stand out from the world we live in by doing everything "without complaining or arguing", and by being "blameless and pure".

■ We cannot work *for* our salvation – Jesus already has.

■ As we obey Christ, our salvation works itself out – becomes visible – in our lives.

■ Timothy and Epaphroditus were working out their salvation, and shining like stars.

■ When people look at our lives, what do they see?

Notes
Philippians 2:12-30

Bible words

The word of life: The message about Jesus. The gospel.
The day of Christ: The day when Jesus Christ will return to judge the world.
Drink offering: An Old Testament offering of wine or water.
Sacrifice: Chosen animals were killed as an offering to God. Sometimes in the Old Testament, a drink offering was poured on top of the sacrifice.

DISCUSS

1. In your own words, what does Paul command in Philippians 2:12?

2. What will it mean in practice for you to "work out your salvation with fear and trembling"?

3. After the challenge of verse 12, why should Paul's next words inspire confidence in his readers?

4. In what ways are you aware of God transforming you or other Christians you know?

5. According to verses 15 and 16, what makes us "shine like stars"?

6. Which do you think is more necessary: to tell people the gospel or to live a godly life among them? Why?

FOLLOW UP

In Philippians 2:12–13, Paul tells the Christians in Philippi to "work out" their salvation. The passages this week explore what that means.

SUNDAY

▣ *Read the passage that will be preached at the church service you attend.*

On the other six days...

DAY ONE

👁 **Re-read Philippians 2:12-30**

▣ *Think about the answers you gave to the questions in Discuss on pages 36-37.*

▣ *Pray that you will be able to "work out your salvation with fear and trembling", thanking God that he is at work in you.*

DAY TWO

👁 **Read Luke 14:25-33**

In this passage, Jesus explains what it will cost to follow him. Jesus is addressing the large crowd who have been travelling with him. He wants them to understand that there is a big difference between being a true follower and just being a spectator.

When Jesus uses the word "hate", he is not telling us, for example, to abandon the commandment to "honour your father and your mother" (Exodus 20:12). He uses such a strong word to show the radical nature of following him. We must always put Christ first.

1. What is involved in being a follower of Jesus, according to verses 26–27?

2. We are to love Jesus more than anything or anyone else. What does this say about who Jesus is?

3. What is the similarity between the man in verses 28–30 and the king in verses 31–32?

➡ In what way are they different?

4. What point is Jesus making with these two stories? (See verse 33.)

Pray that you will become more and more single-minded in following Jesus.

DAY THREE

👁 **Read Galatians 5:16-26**

In this letter, Paul is writing to the churches in Galatia, in modern-day Turkey. His main point in these verses is that in every Christian's life there is a conflict between the Holy Spirit and the sinful nature.

1. There is an important balance in verses 16–18. Our desires lead us in one of two directions. Our aim should be to cooperate with the Holy Spirit and feed that part of our lives – starving the sinful side of us.
   In what areas of your life do you feel the most conflict?

2. Look again at verses 19–21. Are there any things mentioned here which you need to turn from and ask forgiveness for?

   (Note: Some things are obvious actions but others are attitudes that are easier to hide.)

3. Verses 22 and 23 list "the fruit of the Spirit". Which qualities do you particularly need to develop?

4. Paul tells us to "keep in step" with the Spirit (verse 25).
   How can you do this, according to the verses you've just read?

Although it is important that we are aware of the areas in our lives where we need to change, it is also very important that we don't become weighed down by a sense of insurmountable guilt. Remember, God's acceptance of us is based on what *Jesus* has done, not on what *we* have done.

Thank God that "if we confess our sins, he is faithful and just and will forgive us our sins and purify us from all unrighteousness" (1 John 1:9).

DAY FOUR

👁 **Read Romans 12:1-13**

This letter was written by Paul to the Christians in Rome. The "therefore" in 12:1 follows on from the first eleven chapters of Romans, which were a comprehensive explanation of the gospel. In chapter 12, Paul then lays out the practical implications the gospel should have on our lives.

1. What does verse 1 say about what worship is?

2. How is this different from simply singing hymns at church on Sunday?

3. What is the motivation for being "living sacrifices"? (See verse 1.)

4. Verse 2 suggests that our whole way of thinking should change. What will be the result of this change?

5. Verses 3–8 are about using our gifts in the church. In what ways are you currently doing this?

(Note: The list Paul gives in verses 6–8 is not exhaustive.)

6. In verses 9–13 Paul tells us how Christians should behave towards one another. What are these qualities?

Verses 9–13 are very practical. Remembering God's sacrificial love for us helps us to understand how we should love and serve others in the same way.

🔲 *Pray through verses 9-13, asking God to increase your "devotion" and "brotherly love" towards other Christians.*

DAY FIVE

🔲 *Re-read the Bible passages you've read over the past week. Choose a verse that you found particularly helpful, write it down in the space below and memorize it.*

DAY SIX

🔲 *Read Philippians 3:1-9 in preparation for **Discipleship Explored**.*

Do you have any questions about the passages you have read this week?

Summary

In the last session we saw that God is at work in our lives changing both our thoughts and actions, making us more like Jesus. As disciples, we should behave differently to those around us – "shining like stars" as we point them to Jesus.

RIGHTEOUS IN CHRIST

EXPLORE

🔲 *Discuss any questions from last session's Follow Up.*

🔲 *Look together at Philippians 2:19-30 and answer the questions below.*

1. What plans for the future does Paul outline? (See verses 19, 24, 25 and compare with Philippians 1:21–24.)

2. What do we learn about Timothy and his priorities from these verses?

3. How does Paul describe Epaphroditus? What insight do we get into Epaphroditus' attitude and motivation?

4. Why do you think Paul mentions these two men at this point in his letter? (See Philippians 2:4–5.)

5. Paul, Timothy and Epaphroditus all demonstrated their genuine care for fellow believers. In what practical ways can we also do this?

LISTEN

"I consider everything a loss compared to the surpassing greatness of knowing Christ Jesus my Lord." (Philippians 3:8)

Notes
Philippians 3:1-9

- Many people think we can be good enough for God – "righteous" – by doing good things.

- Paul knew that, religiously speaking, he had done everything right. But he described his achievements as "rubbish".

- Our righteousness is like rubbish compared to the righteousness of Jesus.

- Moral or religious "goodness" is nothing compared to "the surpassing greatness of knowing Christ Jesus".

- Our confidence should be in Christ. He is the only one who can make us good enough for God.

- Christ is our righteousness.

Bible words

Circumcision: Cutting off a small piece of skin from the penis. For Jewish people, this was a sign that the man belonged to God's people.

Tribe of Benjamin: All Jews came from one of 12 tribes. Benjamin was one of only two tribes that kept following God.

Hebrew: Another word for Jew.

Pharisees: A group of Jews who followed religious rules and customs very strictly.

1. Paul lists his impressive religious credentials in Philippians 3:5–6. What similar things do people today think will make them right with God?

2. How had Paul's attitude changed and why? (See verses 7 and 8.)

3. What does it mean for us as Christians to "consider everything a loss"?

4. Verse 9 explains what "knowing" or "gaining" Christ means. How would you paraphrase verse 9 to explain it to a non-Christian friend?

5. If we rely on ourselves, what does that show about our view of Jesus Christ?

FOLLOW UP

In Philippians 3:9, Paul speaks about a righteousness that comes as a gift from God and which can be ours through faith. The passages this week explore that theme.

SUNDAY

📖 *Read the passage that will be preached at the church service you attend.*

On the other six days...

DAY ONE

👁 **Re-read Philippians 3:1-9**

📖 *Think about the answers you gave to the questions in Discuss on page 46.*

📖 *Thank God that you have a "righteousness that comes from God and is by faith".*

DAY TWO

👁 **Read Ephesians 2:1-10**

You may remember that we explored part of this passage in Follow Up after Session 1. These verses contain an overview of our salvation.

1. What was our condition before we became Christians? (See verses 1–3.)

2. Why did God do something about our condition? (See verse 4.)

3. Look at your answer to question 1. In what ways did we deserve God's love? (See also Romans 5:8.)

4. So what does Paul mean when he says in Ephesians 2:5, "It is by grace you have been saved"?

5. Why is the distinction between works (verse 9) and faith (verse 8) important to understand?

Pray that you will gain an even clearer understanding of God's grace, so that you can live in the light of it.

DAY THREE

Read Romans 3:20-26

This is one of the most extraordinary passages in the New Testament about what God has done for us through Christ's death.

1. What does "the law" do, according to verse 20?

2. According to the same verse, what will observing the law not do?

3. The word "justification" means being declared "not guilty". How can we, who are guilty, be justified? (See verse 24.)

4. How does this demonstrate both God's justice and his love? (See verses 25–26.)

🔖 *Give thanks to God for his justice and for his love, demonstrated by Jesus' death.*

DAY FOUR

👁 **Read Romans 5:1-11**

In these verses Paul describes the peace and joy that come from being justified.

1. What six statements are true of everyone who has been justified by God?

verse 1:

verse 2:

verse 2 (again):

verse 3:

verse 9:

verse 11:

2. What impact should each of these truths have on your life?

3. According to Paul, what should be our attitude to suffering? Why? (See verses 3–5.)

4. How can we be sure of God's love? (See verses 5 and 8.)

5. Why is the "right answer" to the question "Have you been saved?" both "Yes" and "No"? (See verses 9–10.)

Thank God for the peace you have with him, his presence in your life through the Holy Spirit and the hope of future glory.

DAY FIVE

Re-read the Bible passages you've read over the past week. Choose a verse that you found particularly helpful, write it down in the space below and memorize it.

DAY SIX

*Read Philippians 3:10 – 4:1 in preparation for **Discipleship Explored**.*

Do you have any questions about the passages you have read this week?

Summary

In the last session we saw that keeping religious rules is worthless. It is faith in Christ alone that makes a person right with God.

KNOWING CHRIST

6

EXPLORE

> 📖 *Discuss any questions from last session's Follow Up.*

> 📖 *Look together at Philippians 3:1-4 and answer the questions below.*

1. Why do the Philippians need a safeguard? (See verses 1 and 2.)

2. Some people were teaching that physical circumcision is necessary. Why does Paul say that Christians "are the circumcision"? (See also Romans 2:28–29.)

3. What other marks of the true believer does Paul mention in verse 3?

4. Paul wanted the Philippians to put their confidence in Jesus and in nothing else. Why are Christians sometimes tempted to put their confidence in additional things?

5. What things can we be tempted to rely on in addition to our confidence in Jesus?

6. What should we remember when we are tempted to place confidence in these additional things?

LISTEN

"I want to know Christ and the power of his resurrection and the fellowship of sharing in his sufferings." (Philippians 3:10)

▦ Paul wanted to "know Christ" – better, more deeply, more intimately.

▦ To really know Christ – to walk where he walked – means following the path of suffering.

▦ We should hunger and thirst to know Christ better.

▦ We need to forget what's behind us and press on.

▦ Being a disciple means discipline, including prayer and reading the Bible.

▦ To know Christ we must be heavenly-minded Christians. "Our citizenship is in heaven."

> **Notes**
> Philippians 3:10 – 4:1

Bible words

Attain to the resurrection: Be raised to life by Christ after my death.

DISCUSS

1. In your own words, what is the "one thing" Paul does (according to Philippians 3:12–14), and why?

2. From verses 12–16, what might hinder us from pressing on?

➔ What should encourage us to keep pressing on?

3. In verse 16 Paul says: "Let us live up to what we have already attained". The example of others can help us do this. Why is it important to choose the right role-models? (See verses 17–19.)

4. Look at the phrases in verse 19 that describe those who are "enemies of the cross of Christ". How do people behave in these ways today?

5. What are the sharp contrasts between the descriptions in verse 19 and those in verses 20–21?

6. In the middle of daily life, what does it mean for you to know that your "citizenship is in heaven" and that Christ will return?

FOLLOW UP

In Philippians 3:12–14, Paul declares his determination to "press on" as a Christian. The passages this week will help you think about how you can "press on".

SUNDAY

Read the passage that will be preached at the church service you attend.

On the other six days…

DAY ONE

Re-read Philippians 3:10 – 4:1

Think about the answers you gave to the questions in Discuss on pages 54-55.

Pray that you would be able to keep your focus completely on Jesus Christ.

DAY TWO

Read Matthew 6:19-24

These verses are part of Jesus' preaching known as the "Sermon on the Mount".

1. Jesus tells us to store up "treasures in heaven" rather than "treasures on earth". Why? (See verses 19–20.)

2. What does Jesus mean when he says: "For where your treasure is, there your heart will be also" (verse 21)?

3. How do you invest your time and energy, and what does this show about where your heart is?

4. Jesus says in verse 24 that no one can serve two masters. What competes in your life with serving Jesus?

5. What should you do about that?

Ask God to help you choose treasures that will endure through eternity.

DAY THREE

Read Matthew 6:25-34

This passage carries on from Day Two's reading.

1. What do you learn about God's love for you from verses 26 and 30?

2. According to verse 32, why shouldn't we worry about food or drink or clothing?

3. What should we do instead, according to verse 33?

4. In what practical ways can we do that?

Pray that you would be able to trust God and depend on him for everything.

DAY FOUR

Read Matthew 7:24-29

This parable concludes the Sermon on the Mount.

1. There are two men in this parable. How are they described?

2. There is a similarity and a difference between the two householders. What are they?

3. There are two foundations in this story. What is the difference between them?

4. There are two consequences in this parable. How are they described?

5. What does the storm in verses 25 and 27 symbolize? (See also verses 13, 19 and 23.)

6. Is it enough to listen to Jesus' words? Why or why not?

🔲 *Pray about the areas of your life where you need to put into practice what Jesus teaches here.*

DAY FIVE

📖 *Re-read the Bible passages you've read over the past week. Choose a verse that you found particularly helpful, write it down in the space below and memorize it.*

DAY SIX

📖 *Read Philippians 4:2-9 in preparation for* **Discipleship Explored***.*

Do you have any questions about the passages you have read this week?

Summary

In the last session we saw that we need to press on as disciples of Jesus and stand firm in the Lord. As Christians our "citizenship is in heaven".

REJOICING IN CHRIST

EXPLORE

Discuss any questions from last session's Follow Up.

Look together at Philippians 3:10-11 and answer the questions below.

1. In verse 10, Paul says that his goal is "to know Christ". From verses 10 and 11, what is the challenge that comes from knowing Christ?

2. From verses 10 and 11, what comforts come from knowing Christ?

3. What does Paul mean by wanting to know "the power of his resurrection"? (See also Ephesians 1:17–20.)

4. Can you echo Paul's words in these verses? Why or why not?

LISTEN

"Do not be anxious about anything, but in everything, by prayer and petition, with thanksgiving, present your requests to God."
(Philippians 4:6)

| | Notes |
| | Philippians 4:2-9 |

- Christians should "stand firm *in the Lord*" (Philippians 4:1), "agree with each other *in the Lord*" (verse 2) and "rejoice *in the Lord*" (verse 4).

- The way to be anxious about nothing is to be prayerful about everything.

- The result of praying about everything with thanksgiving is that "the peace of God ... will guard your hearts and your minds in Christ Jesus".

- "The Lord is near" – because as a Christian, his Spirit lives in you; and because he will return soon.

- As Christians, we should fill our minds with excellent and praiseworthy things.

- If we want a life of rejoicing instead of a life of anxiety, we must put these things into practice.

Bible words

Loyal yokefellow: True friend.
The book of life: This symbolizes the fact that God knows every person who has been and will be saved through Jesus Christ.

DISCUSS

1. Do you think Paul is being unrealistic to say "Rejoice in the Lord always" (Philippians 4:4)? Why or why not?

2. When we find it hard to rejoice, what practical steps can we take to help us "rejoice always"?

3. Why will knowing that "the Lord is near" (verse 5) help us to be gentle?

4. What action should we take when we are anxious, and why? (See verses 6–7.)

5. What does it mean to pray "with thanksgiving" (verse 6)? What does this help us to guard against?

FOLLOW UP

The passages this week will help you find out more about prayer.

SUNDAY

Read the passage that will be preached at the church service you attend.

On the other six days...

DAY ONE

👁 Re-read Philippians 4:2-9

Think about the answers you gave to the questions in Discuss on page 64.

Remembering verse 6, pray about the things that make you anxious.

DAY TWO

👁 Read Matthew 6:5-15

Jesus teaches his disciples about prayer.

1. In verses 5–8, what are the contrasts between hypocritical or pagan prayer and the way Jesus says we are to pray?

2. What is Jesus emphasizing about the father-child relationship in verses 5–8?

(Note: Notice how often Jesus uses the word "Father".)

3. We pray to our heavenly Father (verse 9). What are the first things that Jesus tells the disciples to pray? (See verses 9–10?)

(Note: "Hallowed" means "revered" or "honoured".)

4. Why should we pray for these things first?

5. Go through the rest of the prayer phrase by phrase.
What is Jesus teaching us about prayer in each phrase?

6. Look at Jesus' conclusion in verses 14 and 15.
If our lives are not characterized by forgiveness, what does that suggest about our relationship with God?

Use Jesus' prayer as a model for your own prayer.

DAY THREE
Read Colossians 1:3-14

Paul is writing from prison to the church in Colosse, in modern-day Turkey.

1. What does Paul thank God for when he prays for the Christians in Colosse? (See verses 3–4.)

2. Where does the Colossians' faith and love come from? (See verse 5.)

3. What is the main thing Paul prays for the Colossians? (See verse 9.)

4. Why does he pray for this? (See verses 10–12.)

Think of Christians you would like to pray for; then use these verses as a model for your prayers.

DAY FOUR

👁 **Read Colossians 4:2-6**

Here we get an insight into the prayers Paul would like prayed for him.

1. What do we learn from verse 2 about the way we should pray?

2. Given the reason that Paul is in prison (see the end of verse 3), why is Paul's request in verse 3 surprising?

3. How can verses 3 and 4 help you pray for other Christians who want to tell their friends about Jesus?

4. What advice does Paul give about how we should act towards non-Christians? (See verses 5 and 6.)

🔲 *Pray for your effectiveness, and the effectiveness of others, in proclaiming the gospel.*

DAY FIVE

🔲 *Re-read the Bible passages you've read over the past week. Choose a verse that you found particularly helpful, write it down in the space below and memorize it.*

DAY SIX

🔲 *Read Philippians 4:10-23 in preparation for **Discipleship Explored**.*

Do you have any questions about the passages you have read this week?

Summary

In the last session we saw that, as disciples, we should agree in the Lord, rejoice in the Lord, pray to the Lord and think in a way that pleases the Lord.

CONTENT IN CHRIST

EXPLORE

🔲 *Discuss any questions from last session's Follow Up.*

🔲 *Look together at Philippians 4:8-9 and answer the questions below.*

1. What should we spend our time thinking about, according to verse 8?

2. Write down the opposites of all the descriptive words Paul uses in verse 8.

➡ If you were to dwell on such things, what effect would it have on you?

3. On a typical day, what things tend to preoccupy our minds?

4. What incentive is there to do what Paul says? (See verse 9.)

5. How will you act upon Paul's command in verse 8?

LISTEN

"I have learned the secret of being content in any and every situation."
(Philippians 4:12)

■ Many people believe that the secret
of contentment is to change your
circumstances.

■ Paul says he has learned to be content
whatever the circumstances.

■ The source of contentment is Christ.

■ Paul says: "I can do everything through
him who gives me strength". This
means that in every circumstance God
gives him the strength to be content.

■ We can trust God with everything: our
time, money, career, family, future and
life.

■ God will meet all our needs "according
to his glorious riches in Christ Jesus".

> ### Notes
> Philippians 4:10-23

Bible words

Macedonia: Philippi was in Macedonia, part of ancient Greece.
Thessalonica: Another city in Macedonia.
Amen: A Hebrew word which means "certainly" or "so be it".

DISCUSS

1. In what ways does society tempt us to be discontent?

2. Paul says that he has "learned the secret of being content in any and every situation". Where does Paul find true contentment, according to Philippians 4:13? (See also 4:7–9, 1:21 and 3:10–11.)

3. What practical steps can you take in order to be content in "any and every situation"?

4. What do verses 14–18 tell us about the generosity shown by the Christians in Philippi?

5. How should we "share in the troubles" of fellow Christians today?

6. Does verse 19 mean that Christians will never be in financial difficulty? Why or why not?

7. What is encouraging about the way Paul ends his letter? (See verses 20–23.)

FOLLOW UP

Paul ends his letter to the Philippians by speaking about contentment. The passages this week will help you to see how this is possible.

SUNDAY

Read the passage that will be preached at the church service you attend.

On the other six days...

DAY ONE
Re-read Philippians 4:10-23

Think about the answers you gave to the questions in Discuss on pages 72-73.

Pray that you would learn to be "content in any and every situation".

DAY TWO
Read Hebrews 4:14-16

This short passage gives us great assurance.

1. Why should we hold "firmly" to the faith we profess (verse 14)?

2. What do you consider to be your particular weaknesses and temptations (verse 15)?

3. What should we do in times of weakness and temptation? (See verses 15–16.)

4. How will God respond if we do this? (See verse 16.)

Use your answers to these questions to help you pray.

DAY THREE

👁 Read 1 Timothy 1:12-17

Paul wrote two letters to his younger colleague, Timothy. Here Paul talks about his sense of unworthiness because he used to persecute Christians.

1. What does Paul thank Jesus for in verse 12?

2. What did Paul receive from Jesus (verse 14)?

3. Why is the "saying" in verse 15 so fundamental for Paul and for us?

4. How was Paul's life an example of God's patience? (See verses 13 and 16.)

5. How is your life an example of God's patience to those who aren't yet Christians? (See verse 16.)

6. In verse 12, Paul mentions that Jesus gave him strength.
In what ways have you too received strength from Jesus?

🖺 *Pray about your witness as a Christian in the places where you work and live. Ask for God's strength to live for him and to be ready to tell others about Jesus.*

DAY FOUR
👁 Read Ephesians 3:14-21

This prayer is right in the middle of Paul's letter to the Christians in Ephesus, in Ancient Greece. In it, he prays that they would have "power".

1. What is the first thing Paul prays for the Ephesians? (See verses 16–17a.)

2. What is required from the Ephesians to make this prayer effective (verse 17a)?

3. The Ephesians are already Christians, and therefore already have Christ living in them. So what does Paul mean when he prays that Christ would "dwell" in them?

4. What is the second thing Paul prays for the Ephesians? (See verses 17b–19.)

5. How can the "love" that Paul mentions in verse 19 be known, but at the same time "surpass knowledge"?

6. What is it about the end of Paul's prayer that encourages us to pray? (See verse 20.)

Use these verses to pray for yourself and all Christians everywhere, that we would grow in our knowledge of the love of Jesus.

DAY FIVE

Re-read the Bible passages you've read over the past week.
Choose a verse that you found particularly helpful, write it down in the space below and memorize it.

DAY SIX

🔲 *Now that you've finished* **Discipleship Explored***, spend some time writing down the things you have learned. Pray that you will be able to put them into practice.*

THE WEEKS AHEAD

Paul wants the Philippians to experience "progress and joy in the faith" (Philippians 1:25). Our prayer for you is the same.

The first thing a believer must do is join a church. The local church is where Christians receive baptism and the Lord's Supper (also known as Communion or the Eucharist), showing the whole world that they belong to Jesus' kingdom now (Ephesians 3:10-11). The local church is where Christians grow in the knowledge of God's word, teaching and being taught, discipling and being discipled.

You will also want to continue your own daily Bible reading. (The book of James is a great follow-up to *Discipleship Explored*.)

"Finally ... whatever is true, whatever is noble, whatever is right, whatever is pure, whatever is lovely, whatever is admirable – if anything is excellent or praiseworthy – think about such things."

The background to Philippians

Philippians is a letter from the New Testament. It was written by Paul to a group of Christians living in the city of Philippi, a Roman colony in ancient Greece.

Paul and Timothy visited Philippi to tell people about Jesus (see Acts 16:11-40). They were forced to leave after a short time because the city rulers did not want them to cause any trouble. They left behind them a small group of new Christians. Paul wrote this letter to them from prison in Rome. He wanted to:

➔ encourage the new Christians in Philippi

➔ help them keep going as Christians in difficult times

➔ remind them about the good news of Jesus Christ

➔ give them practical instructions on what it means to live as a follower of Christ. That is what "disciple" means – a learner, a follower.

You may have recently made a decision to become a Christian. You may be still thinking about what it means to follow Jesus. Or you may be someone who has been a Christian for years, and you want to go over the basics once again.

Whoever you are, this short letter will help you understand how good it is to be a follower of Jesus Christ, and how he calls his disciples to live for him today.

WHO WAS PAUL?

Paul was originally called Saul. As a devoted Jew, he hated the first Jewish Christians and put many of them in prison. But while travelling to Damascus, he was stopped by a bright light and heard Jesus Christ speaking to him (Acts 9). This experience changed Paul completely. He became a Christian and was sent by Jesus to be a teacher and leader.

Paul travelled a lot around southern Europe and Asia, telling others about Jesus Christ. He organised the new disciples into churches, and wrote letters to them, teaching them and encouraging them to keep going. He was often persecuted himself, and was eventually executed by the Romans.

Many of Paul's letters are now in the New Testament. Philippians is one of them.

Map

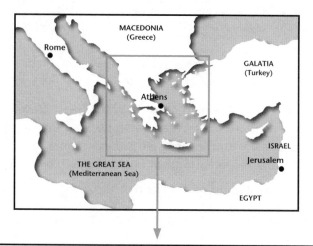